WASHOE COUNTY LIBRARY

3 1235 03403 4293

P9-CJI-714

Family Crises

By Jillian Powell

Health Consultant: John G. Samanich, M.D.

 **Gareth Stevens**
Publishing
A WEEKLY READER COMPANY

Please visit our web site at www.garethstevens.com.
For a free color catalog describing Gareth Stevens
Publishing's list of high-quality books, call
1-800-542-2595 (USA) or 1-800-387-3178 (Canada).
Gareth Stevens Publishing's fax: 1-877-542-2596

Library of Congress Cataloging-in-Publication Data
Powell, Jillian.
   Family crises / Jillian Powell; health consultant, John G.
Samanich.
      p. cm. — (Emotional health issues)
   Includes bibliographical references and index.
   ISBN-13: 978-0-8368-9201-7 (lib. bdg.)
   ISBN-10: 0-8368-9201-1 (lib. bdg.)
   1. Family—Juvenile literature.   2. Crises—Juvenile
literature.   I. Samanich, John G.   II. Title.
HQ734.P834   2009
158.2'4—dc22   2008005460

The information in this
book is not intended to
substitute for professional
medical or psychological
care. The case studies are
based on real experiences,
but the names are fictitious.
All people in the photos are
models except where a
caption specifically names
an individual.

This North American edition first published in 2009 by
Gareth Stevens Publishing
A Weekly Reader® Company
1 Reader's Digest Road
Pleasantville, NY 10570-7000 USA

This U.S. edition copyright © 2009 by Gareth Stevens, Inc.
Original edition copyright © 2008 by Wayland. First published in Great Britain in 2008
by Wayland, 338 Euston Road, London NW1 3BH, United Kingdom.

Series Editor: Nicola Edwards   Consultant: Peter Evans
Designer: Alix Wood   Picture Researcher: Kathy Lockley

Gareth Stevens Managing Editor: Lisa M. Herrington
Gareth Stevens Senior Editor: Barbara Bakowski
Gareth Stevens Creative Director: Lisa Donovan

Photo credits: ClassicStock/H. Armstrong Roberts/Alamy: 4; Ned Frisk Photography/Corbis: 5;
Nick Kennedy/Alamy: 7; Joanne O'Brien/Photofusion: 18; Photodisc/SW Productions/Alamy:
Cover, 10; Paula Solloway/Photofusion: 6; Wishlist: title page, 8, 9, 11-17, 20-45; Wolf/zefa/Corbis: 19

All rights reserved. No part of this book may be reproduced, stored in a retrieval system, or transmitted
in any form or by any means, electronic, mechanical, photocopying, recording, or otherwise, without
the prior written permission of the copyright holder.

Printed in China
1 2 3 4 5 6 7 8 9 10 09 08

Contents

Words that appear in **boldface** type are in the glossary on page 46.

Introduction

Josh is running away. This is not the first time he has left home, but this time he intends to stay away. His family troubles began a few years ago, when his parents divorced. Now Josh always seems to be arguing with his mother, and the fighting has become worse since she married Greg. Josh's stepfather **bullies** him and has even threatened him with violence. Greg hits Josh's mom, too. Josh doesn't want to live with his mom and Greg any longer, so he has decided to leave home. His family is in crisis.

Changes in the family

Families are changing. Two generations ago, most children lived in families with two parents. Today there are many more single-parent families and **blended families** than there were in the past. Single parents may be divorced or separated, or they may never have married. Blended families result when one or both parents find new partners. Some children are brought up by two parents of the same sex. Others are brought up by grandparents or in **foster families**.

Blended families

If a parent experiences divorce or **bereavement** and later remarries, children may have to adjust to living with a stepparent and stepsiblings. Sometimes, this situation is difficult. Young people may resent a stepparent

In the 1950s and 1960s, most families were made up of a married couple living with their children.

for taking a natural parent's place. Some children and teens feel jealous of a stepparent and stepsiblings. Children may also feel guilty about being part of a stepfamily if their other parent is alone. Young people can have trouble adjusting to new ways of doing things. There may be disagreements, especially if stepsiblings have to share rooms and belongings.

It's a fact:
family life

- There are about 13 million single-parent households in the United States.
- One-third of U.S. children under the age of 18 live with one parent.
- Four out of five single parents are mothers.
- About 8 percent of children live in a household that includes a grandparent.

Although some children adjust to new family settings, others may go on feeling unhappy and lonely. This can lead to **depression** and stress-related illnesses that affect their lives at home and at school.

Impact on children

Many children experience change and upheaval as they are growing up. They may face family crises that challenge their physical and mental well-being. An increase in the number of children with emotional, mental, and behavioral disorders reflects the more intense stresses in modern family life.

Find out more

The following chapters present the facts about family crises. Find out about the circumstances and events that can cause stress, conflict, and unhappiness within families. Learn about the effects that family problems can have on young people's feelings and lives. Find advice on seeking support, and get information about available resources. You will learn that people can overcome problems and find means of surviving and recovering from family crises.

Many children today grow up in single-parent families.

5

Chapter 1: *Changing lifestyles*

There have been significant changes in society during the last few decades. Fifty years ago, most people stayed and worked in the area where they were born. **Extended families** (which may include grandparents, uncles, and aunts) were often close at hand to provide support, advice, and child care. Today people are more mobile, often moving away from their families to work. Traditional family support systems have changed. In the past, young parents could turn to their own parents or grandparents for help and advice. Now family members may be separated by distance, and some lose contact.

Work and child care

Family lifestyles have also changed greatly in recent decades. In the past, most mothers stayed at home to care for their children while the fathers went out to work to earn money. Today people's working patterns have changed. In some families, the mother is the main wage earner while the father looks after the children and the home. In many families, both parents work outside the home. More than 70 percent of American women with children under age 18 work outside the home—including 60 percent of

Children with working parents may have to rely on meals heated up in a microwave if their parents are busy.

6

mothers with children under age three.

Lifestyle changes may mean that parents spend less time with their children. Some families rely on grandparents, nannies, babysitters, day-care centers, or after-school programs for child care. According to a 2005 report by the U.S. Census Bureau, about 63 percent of children under age five were regularly in some type of child care.

Fast-food meals

Eating habits have also changed. Few families regularly sit down to share meals. Today many children grab

In focus: the impact of technology

Technology has changed home life so that family members spend less time interacting with and talking to one another. For example, when televisions first came into family homes in the 1950s, families gathered to watch favorite shows together. Today many children have their own TV sets and watch alone in their bedrooms while other family members watch television in another room.

Children may also spend a lot of time at home alone, playing handheld video games, using computers, text-messaging friends on cell phones, or listening to music on digital audio players.

a cereal bar to eat on the way to school. In the evening, they may have a fast-food meal or eat alone in front of a TV rather than at the family table.

Because of changes in work and life patterns, modern families live more separate lives than those of the past. In a time of crisis, such as a serious illness, a bereavement, or a divorce, families may have trouble working out the problems together.

For many modern families, watching TV is no longer a shared activity.

Chapter 2: *Family breakup*

Family breakup happens when parents separate or divorce. It is one of the most stressful events a family can experience. Divorce affects every member of the family, including parents, children, grandparents, and other close relatives.

Life changes

In recent decades, divorce has become much more common than in the past. Many couples decide to split up because they no longer love each other or because they have grown apart and want different things from life. Some meet new partners and decide to remarry.

When parents divorce, their children often face major life changes. Families must decide, sometimes with the help of a court, which parent will have **custody** of the children. Some children live part of the time with one parent, part with the other. Some young people live mainly with one parent and visit the other regularly. Some children see the absent parent only occasionally or not at all.

While many parents cooperate with each other after a divorce,

After a family breakup, children may have to adapt to a new routine, such as spending alternate weeks with different parents.

If a divorced parent moves away, a child may communicate mainly through e-mail and telephone calls.

some divorced parents are hostile. Children may lose contact with grandparents and other relatives from one side of the family. This situation can be difficult for everyone involved. In extreme cases, a parent who has been denied custody may illegally take a child away to live with him or her.

One or both parents may find new partners and remarry. If they do so, the children have to adjust to a blended family, living part-time or full-time with a new stepparent and possibly stepsiblings. When families break up, it can mean a move for one or both parents to a new house or even to a new city or state. Children and teenagers may need to change schools and make new friends, bringing more upheaval in their lives. The changes brought about by divorce can be stressful for all members of the family.

It's a fact:
marriage and divorce

- In the United States, 43 percent of first marriages end in divorce within 15 years.

- According to a report by the Centers for Disease Control and Prevention, divorce can have harmful effects on the health and well-being of children. It is linked to more health problems and more risky behaviors, such as increased alcohol use.

The impact of family breakup

Separation and divorce can create a great deal of tension within a family. Parents may argue constantly or may not talk to each other at all. Because some family members feel stressed and irritable, they are unusually impatient and snap at others.

Some children hear their parents say hurtful things. Young people may even witness violence between their parents. Children may feel afraid for a parent's safety and may worry that they are in danger, too.

Taking the blame

Some children and teens do not understand why their parents cannot get along as they used to. Children may believe that the divorce is somehow their fault— that it is the result of something they have done or not done. They may hope that they can reunite their parents.

Children may worry about where they will live and whether they will see a parent who is moving out of the family home. Young people sometimes feel forced to "take sides" with one parent against the other, complicating their feelings of hurt and confusion.

Arguments and conflict can make children feel torn and confused.

Experiencing loss

Children experience many difficult emotions during a family breakup— sadness, anger, **anxiety**, fear, and embarrassment. There is often an overwhelming sense of loss and a yearning for how things used to be in the family.

Preteens and teenagers often focus on the moral issues surrounding divorce. They may be judgmental of their parents' decisions and actions. Many teens become anxious about their own future relationships.

A child may find it hard to concentrate in class or to do homework because of his or her worries and distractions. These concerns can have a negative effect on a child's performance at school. In time, however, most children adapt to the new family situation, and their grades improve.

Young people may be unable to concentrate on schoolwork when their emotions are in turmoil.

CASE STUDY

Dawn's parents were always arguing. From her bedroom, she could hear their fights. Their voices were always angry and loud. Sometimes Dawn sat on the stairs and cried because she felt so worried.

One day Dawn's parents told her and her sister that they were getting a divorce. Their dad moved out the next weekend. Dawn felt heartbroken. She hated her parents' fights, but she didn't want her dad to leave. She felt worse when she didn't see her dad on special days, such as her birthday, even though he always called in the evening. Dawn desperately hoped that her mother and father would get back together again. After a few months, she found out that her dad was in a relationship with another woman. Dawn realized then that her parents would not reconcile.

She felt better after talking to her friend Elena, whose parents had divorced a few years earlier. Elena told Dawn that she would feel better in time. Elena also reminded Dawn that her mom and dad loved her.

Working it out

Children are sometimes unable to talk openly about their feelings during a family breakup. They may be worried that they will cause more trouble and anger between their parents. Young people may also feel pressure to side with one parent or the other in a conflict. Some children feel angry and let down by their parents. They may react by becoming rebellious and acting out in destructive ways. Some young people respond by withdrawing emotionally from their parents and family life.

Depression

Many children and teens become anxious and depressed during and after a family breakup. Depression can result when a young person feels that he or she is powerless to change or control a situation.

Children may feel particularly upset on special occasions, such as birthdays, holidays, or other family celebrations. They may experience behavioral problems at school and at home.

Talking therapies

Children need to talk about how they feel if they are to come to terms with family breakup. They need to discuss what they are going through and how it is affecting them. Young people can talk to teachers or school **counselors** to make them aware of the home situation and why their schoolwork may be affected.

Some children may need to meet with child or family counselors, **therapists**, or **social workers**. These professionals can help children understand their

Teachers can offer support and understanding during a student's family crisis.

emotions and and cope with their family life. At divorce recovery support groups, children can meet and talk with other young people who are experiencing the same problems and feelings. Children and teens can also get advice and support by calling telephone helplines.

Coping strategies

Certain strategies can help children cope during a family breakup. Young people should keep to familiar routines, especially in arrangements for seeing absent parents. Maintaining contact with other relatives, such as grandparents, and with family pets can provide stability and comfort.

Keeping a diary may help teens express their feelings. Exercise is beneficial, too. Physical activity produces **endorphins**, chemicals in the brain that boost mood. Trying a new activity or sport can be a distraction and can help young people feel excitement instead of despair and loss.

In focus: child custody

Some parents easily agree on arrangements for custody of their children. If parents can't agree, however, a court may decide custody. An official may talk to the children and their parents and then make a report to the court. The court considers the children's physical, educational, and emotional needs. The court also looks at the parents' fitness and other factors that affect the welfare of the children.

Courts usually weigh children's custody preferences differently according to their age. Some children have divided loyalties. They may worry that their decision will upset one of their parents. Children need to be assured that their relationship with both parents will stay the same, whatever the living arrangements.

13

Chapter 3: *Bereavement*

The death of a loved one is one of the hardest things anyone can face. Bereavement can bring deep sadness, an aching sense of loss, and a feeling of abandonment. Grief is a normal and natural response to loss. If someone has died suddenly, perhaps from a heart attack or in a traffic accident, shock and disbelief are natural reactions. When there has been no time for good-byes, children sometimes feel guilty about things they have said or not said or about their recent behavior. They may feel guilt more keenly if a parent or a sibling has died by suicide. In the case of a **terminal illness**, a long period of stress and anxiety may have preceded the death. Children may have missed out on family life and fun or have had to be more self-sufficient because of the family situation.

Feeling isolated

Children who have lost a parent or a sibling can feel very **isolated**. They may not know others who have been bereaved in the same way. Young people may feel awkward or embarrassed among their **peers** because they think their loss makes them "different." They believe that nobody understands their feelings. Some children face difficult questions about what has happened to them. Friends who are uncomfortable or who don't know what to say may avoid the bereaved person.

Children who have experienced the death of a parent or a sibling can feel isolated from their friends.

Coping with emotions

Many children struggle to cope when they are hurting inside. They may put on a brave face because they don't want to cause grieving family members more worry. Young people may feel angry and resentful about the changes that bereavement has caused in their lives. They may believe that there is little point in doing schoolwork or any of the activities they used to enjoy.

The loss of a close relative can leave young people feeling anxious about their own death or the deaths of other family members. Some children experience physical symptoms, such as headaches and stomach pain. Teens may withdraw from social life. They are more likely to engage in risky behaviors, such as alcohol and drug abuse or reckless driving.

The feelings of shock, distress, and bitterness that follow a loved one's death may persist for months. Young people may feel hopeless and become depressed. Through counseling, these people can be helped to come to terms with their grief and move forward.

It's a fact: bereavement

- In the United States, about 3 percent of children under the age of 18 experience the death of a parent.
- Almost 90 percent of students face the death of a sibling, another relative, or a close friend before finishing high school.
- Children and teenagers are most likely to experience problems in the first year after bereavement. One in ten young people experiences depression.

The loss of a grandparent may be a child's first experience of bereavement.

Facing changes

The death of a parent can bring many changes to a child's life. Some children continue to live with the surviving parent, sometimes with the help of additional child care. Some young people are cared for by grandparents or other close relatives.

When a parent dies, a child may feel that his or her role within the family has changed. A son who loses his father, for example, may feel he is now the "man of the house." He takes on more responsibility for his mother and siblings.

The death of a brother or sister can also bring changes in family relationships. Surviving siblings may have difficult and confused feelings. They may feel neglected by grieving parents. Initial feelings of resentment are often followed by shame or guilt.

Losing a grandparent is painful for many children. A grandparent's death can mean the loss of a trusted listener,

When a parent dies, older children may have to care for younger siblings.

adviser, and supporter. For many children, the loss of a grandparent can be the first experience of death. If a grandparent has been ill, there may be a sense of relief at the end of suffering, but guilt and deep sorrow can follow.

Children and teens are also deeply affected by the death of a close friend. When a peer dies, for example from an illness or an accident, young people may experience shock and denial. Then they often feel bewildered, angry, insecure, frightened, and out of control. Children and teens sometimes express their anger in destructive ways.

A pet's death can cause strong and painful feelings, too. Pets are often an important part of the family, and their loss can leave a huge gap in a young person's life.

CASE STUDY

Jake was nine when his father died suddenly following a heart attack. Jake felt as if his whole world had fallen apart. His dad had seemed so healthy and fit, and they had often played football together. Jake's sister was too young to understand, and Jake felt it was up to him to look after his mother. He couldn't bear to see her sad. He worried constantly that she would become ill or that something bad would happen to her. Jake tried to hide his sorrow and fears for his mom's sake, but he often cried himself to sleep.

Jake's teacher noticed his distress and talked to his mother. Jake's mom arranged for him to go to a weekend bereavement camp, where he met other children who had lost a parent. At first Jake found it hard to talk about his dad. As he listened to the other campers talk about their losses, he realized they would understand his feelings. Jake was helped by sharing his emotions with other young people who had experienced a loss similar to his own.

Some people find comfort in visiting the grave of a loved one.

Healing and recovery

Many people need extra help and support to help them cope following a bereavement. When a person dies suddenly, families often receive immediate support from hospital staff. **Hospices** can give support when a death has been expected due to illness.

Some people find that in the immediate aftermath of a death, they feel a numbness that helps them manage the many tasks that have to be done. Friends and neighbors help inform people and offer support as families arrange for funerals.

It is only later, when funerals are over and other people have returned to their normal routines, that bereaved families struggle to cope with their loss. They may feel that others expect them to accept their losses and show signs of recovery.

Counseling and therapy

People may find it difficult to talk about their loss, especially if a death resulted from suicide. It is important to know, however, that talking is a vital part of healing. Children are sometimes afraid that they will forget the person who has died. It is important that young people have opportunities to remember their loved one, talk about him or her, and express their emotions. Teachers, school counselors, doctors, social workers, and therapists can listen and provide information and support. Some schools arrange for bereaved students to have access to a counselor during the school day.

Peer support groups

Many bereavement organizations offer peer support groups so that young people who have lost a

School counselors can help students share their feelings of loss and identify ways of coping with grief.

Good-bye ceremonies include actions such as releasing a balloon for a person who has died. These rituals can aid in the healing process after the loss of a loved one.

loved one can meet with children and teens who are experiencing the same difficult emotions.

Children express their grief through their behavior, emotions, physical reactions, and thoughts. Support groups provide safe and comfortable environments in which young people can talk about their experiences. They may discuss changes in their home life, new roles or expectations within the family, and concerns about the future.

Young people's confidence is often damaged by the loss of security, trust, and control that bereavement brings. Peer support groups can help restore **self-esteem**. Meeting other young people who are grieving can change group members' perspectives and provide a valuable step toward healing.

In focus: bereavement camps

Organizations such as Camp Angel Wings, Comfort Zone Camp, and Camp ReLeaf offer programs for children who have lost a loved one. Children take part in **therapeutic** activities such as such balloon release or candle-lighting ceremonies. Healing projects can include the making of memory books or collages. Group discussions provide opportunities for young people to express feelings of anger, pain, and resentment. Trained staff, peers in a similar situation, and coping activities help young people deal with grief and move toward healing.

Chapter 4: *Young caregivers*

Some young people must care for a family member who has an illness, a disability, or an **addiction** to drugs or alcohol. These young caregivers take on responsibilities that would normally fall to an adult. Because of the recent rise in the number of single-parent families in the United States, however, more than 1 million children are responsible for the care of ill or disabled parents, siblings, or other relatives. Many children must care for younger siblings, too, because their parents are unable to do so. Most young caregivers are from eight to 18 years old, according to a national study by the National Alliance for Caregiving.

Physical and emotional care

Most young caregivers look after parents or grandparents with illnesses such as **Alzheimer's disease** and cancer. Other adults who need care may have heart, lung, or kidney disease. Some have arthritis or diabetes. Some young people have to help a family member who is coping with an addiction to drugs or alcohol. Other caregivers need to support a relative with a mental illness.

Supporting a parent with a mental illness or an addiction can be physically and emotionally draining for a young person.

These children and teens give physical care, such as helping a family member get dressed,

Many young caregivers struggle to complete schoolwork, carry out household tasks, and look after younger siblings.

Caring for siblings

Children with a sibling who is ill or who has a disability may have to stay at home often to help provide care. Young caregivers often assist with feeding and bathing. They may also have to look after themselves much of the time, because their siblings require a great deal of their parents' time and attention.

Coping with crises

Some young caregivers have to deal with upsetting and challenging situations. These children have to act as caregivers because their parents are feeding and bathing the person, and giving medication. Care may involve lifting an adult in and out of bed.

Young caregivers usually do household jobs, too, such as cooking and cleaning. Almost all young caregivers help with shopping and meal preparation. About three-fourths of young caregivers get some help. Half of them, however, say they spend a lot of time each day performing household and caregiving tasks.

It's a fact:
young caregivers

- In the United States, more than 1.3 million children and teens care for an ill or disabled family member.
- About 400,000 caregivers are under the age of 12.
- Among caregivers ages eight to 18, more than one-third care for a grandparent. Another third care for a parent, and 11 percent care for a sibling.

Young caregivers typically spend more time indoors than their peers do. Children and teens who care for family members may envy friends who have more freedom and who enjoy more carefree lifestyles.

unable to care for a home and family. Some parents abuse drugs or alcohol. Alcohol and drugs can alter behavior and lead people to take dangerous risks or to behave in an irrational, angry, or aggressive way. A parent may take a **drug overdose**, accidentally or intentionally. Some parents **binge drink**, consuming several alcoholic drinks within a short time. They may lose consciousness. In these circumstances, children need to call emergency service providers, such as police or **paramedics**.

Other parents may have an addiction to gambling. Relatives sometimes go to great lengths to keep people outside the family from knowing about the problems. A parent's addiction can become a "family secret" that a child feels compelled to keep.

Some parents turn to crime to pay for their addictions. The effects on their families can be devastating. Crime can result in arrest, conviction, and imprisonment. Debt can cause families to fall behind in rent or mortgage payments and eventually lose a home or face **eviction**.

CASE STUDY

Sara was 12 when her mother became ill. Sara had to help around the house, doing the dishes, cooking meals, and looking after her younger brother Luis and sister Rosa. Sara got up early every day to make breakfast and to help Luis and Rosa dress for school. Sara also gave her mom her medication. After school, Sara cared for Luis and Rosa, making sure they did their homework and tidied up their rooms. Sara cleaned the house and cooked dinner before doing her own homework and getting her brother and sister ready for bed.

Sara was often tired at school, but she didn't want to ask for help. She was afraid that school officials would report her mother to child protective services for neglect. Sara missed a lot of school and dropped out when she was 16.

Problems faced by young caregivers

Children and teenagers who are full-time caregivers often experience stress and anxiety. They worry about the future and what will happen if their parent or sibling dies. Young caregivers are sometimes reluctant to leave the people they care for and to take time out for themselves. They may be angry or resentful about their role and may feel unappreciated. This, in turn, can cause feelings of guilt.

Young caregivers often get up early and go to bed late because they must do many household tasks before and after school.

Young caregivers have to deal with many other problems, too, such as frustration and fatigue. They may have to make many personal sacrifices, giving up time with friends and missing out on social and recreational activities. Depression, mood swings, and **antisocial behavior** are more common among teenage caregivers than their peers.

Some young people begin to **self-harm**. Self-harm can be a young caregiver's way of seeking control over his or her life.

School and education

Surveys have found that as many as one in three young caregivers has problems at school. Getting to school on time can be hard. Some students miss school because they are worried about leaving a parent or a sibling alone at home.

One in five young caregivers has missed a school activity or an after-school activity. About 15 percent of students say their responsibilities at home have kept them from doing schoolwork and have affected their grades. Young caregivers are more likely than their peers to have trouble getting along with teachers, to bully other students, and to have behavior problems at school.

Isolated and ashamed

Many young people who care for their parents or other relatives feel isolated. They may also feel confused, hurt, and disappointed or betrayed by a parent whom they love and need.

Children who must care for adult relatives are often embarrassed to tell others what is happening at home. Some young caregivers have to deal with bullying or hurtful remarks about their families from other children.

Some young caregivers have to cope with bullying and taunts from peers.

If a parent loses consciousness, a young caregiver must seek medical help immediately. Emergency service providers can offer advice and will stay on the line until an ambulance crew arrives at the scene.

Support for young caregivers

Experts say there is a "hidden army" of child caregivers in the United States. As many as three-quarters of all young caregivers are unknown to social services or to teachers and other adults in authority.

Many child caregivers live in single-parent homes, with only the ill or disabled parent. In two-parent households, the healthy parent may be working. Many families cannot

It's a fact: parents with addictions

- According to the National Household Survey on Drug Abuse, more than 6 million American children live with a parent who has a drug or alcohol abuse problem.

- Alcohol abuse is closely linked with **domestic violence**.

- Nearly one-half of child neglect and abuse cases are associated with a parent's abuse of alcohol or drugs.

- "Casino kids" may be left in parking lots for hours while their parents gamble.

afford paid home-care help. Some children fear that if they seek help, they will be removed from their parents and taken into foster care. These young caregivers need to know that help and support are available.

Getting help

Young caregivers need emotional support. If they do not feel able to approach anyone in person, they can call a helpline for immediate advice and assistance. Some organizations specialize in helping children whose parents have addiction problems. Through Alateen, for example, young people can share experiences, discuss their difficulties, and learn ways to cope with their problems.

Young caregiver projects

The American Association for Caregiving Youth (AACY) helps preteens and teens through local caregiving youth projects. Students are offered in-school counseling, support groups, caregiving breaks, and outside activities. Young caregivers can also receive links to organizations that provide transportation, medical care, meals, and tutoring services.

Dealing with feelings

Young caregivers have to deal with many difficult feelings and emotions. One way of coping with painful feelings is to write them in a journal

Young caregivers can benefit from talking to other teens with similar problems and family situations.

Writing in a journal can be a form of therapy. It is important for young caregivers to find ways to express painful emotions.

or express them in a poem, a drawing, or a painting. Children and teens can relieve stress and frustration by practicing deep-breathing and other relaxation techniques.

Taking a break

Caring for someone who needs a lot of help with daily activities can be frustrating, challenging, lonely, and sometimes overwhelming. Young people need occasional breaks from their caregiving responsibilities. Periodic breaks can help caregivers relax for a while and return to their tasks with renewed energy. Young caregivers should make sure they plan some time in the day for their own interests and enjoyment, such as listening to music, participating in a sport, reading, playing a video game, or watching television.

In focus: online help

The National Alliance for Caregiving (**www.caregiving.org**) offers online resources to help people care for their loved ones. Brochures, checklists, links, and a message board give caregivers the basic tools and information they need. The Family Caregiving 101 web site (**www.familycaregiving101.org**) offers valuable tips on meeting the challenges of caregiving.

Chapter 5: *Prison, violence, and abuse*

Families can be hit hard by crises such as debt or imprisonment. When a parent goes to prison, a child may have reactions similar to those of bereavement—shock, loss, and grief. Children who were present during a parent's arrest sometimes experience nightmares or **flashbacks** about the experience. Having a family member in prison can bring feelings of shame or embarrassment, and some children face bullying or teasing from peers. Others may become anxious and withdrawn, feel isolated, or have problems at school.

Living arrangements

When a parent goes to prison, family circumstances change. Some families have to move to a different home. Fathers are more likely to be the imprisoned parent—more than 90 percent of imprisoned parents are fathers, and their children generally live with their mothers. If a mother is imprisoned, children are more likely to live with grandparents or other relatives. In some cases, children need to be placed in foster homes. Some families face serious financial hardship due to a loss of income following a parent's imprisonment.

Staying in contact

Many prisoners are held in facilities that are far from their family homes. Long distances and limited visiting

Among children with imprisoned fathers, more than 85 percent live with their mothers.

hours sometimes make it difficult for children to stay in contact with parents in prison. Although prison visits can be stressful and upsetting, experts say most children benefit from seeing their parents. Young people often worry about the parent's well-being, and they need reassurance that the absent parent loves them. Grandparents and other relatives can provide needed stability and care.

Getting support

Children with parents in prison often feel isolated and alone. Several organizations offer support. Some offer group meetings and activities so that children and teens can meet other young people in similar situations. Other organizations offer legal services, transportation for prison visits, counseling, and telephone helplines that children can call for advice and information.

It's a fact:
parents in prison

- In 2006, one in every 31 adults in the United States was in prison or on **probation** or **parole**.

- About 2 million American children have at least one parent in prison, according to the Administration for Children and Families.

- Children with parents in prison are at increased risk for poor school performance, dropping out, gang involvement, mental health problems, drug abuse, and suicide, according to the Child Welfare League of America.

CASE STUDY

Eleven-year-old Joshua was at home when his father was arrested. Josh shut himself in his room and cried for hours. He felt shocked, frightened, and disappointed because his dad had to leave Josh, his mother, and his brothers. Josh wondered how his mother would manage to take care of them and pay the household bills.

He didn't know any other students at school who had a parent in prison. Some kids made hurtful remarks about his dad and called him names. Josh felt angry with his dad but still loved him and worried about him in prison. Josh phoned a helpline because there was no one else he felt he could talk to about his feelings. A worker there put Josh in touch with a group where he could meet other children in the same situation.

Domestic violence

Domestic violence is abusive behavior by one member of a family or household against another. The violence can happen occasionally or frequently. There are many forms of domestic violence, and all of them involve controlling and aggressive behavior. The abuse can be verbal (name-calling), physical (hitting, choking), sexual, emotional, or psychological (threatening or **stalking**).

Domestic violence can happen to anyone, but most victims are women who are abused by their husbands or partners. Conflict within a relationship and the abuse of alcohol or drugs are factors that increase the risk of domestic violence. In homes where domestic violence occurs, children are physically abused and neglected at a rate 15 times higher than the national average.

Witnessing violence

Experts estimate that 3 million children witness violence in their homes each year. Most of them are aware of the abuse. The effects of seeing or hearing domestic violence are similar to the effects of being abused. Young people may feel helpless and frightened. Some of them experience anxiety and sleeplessness.

Children and teens may try to stop the violence, putting themselves in danger. They sometimes feel that they are responsible for their parent's or stepparent's abusive behavior. Children may avoid talking about the violence

Hearing violence at home can lead to stress and anxiety in children and teens. Older siblings often try to protect younger siblings from the effects of domestic violence.

because they don't want to cause more upset in the family. They can feel lonely and isolated, as if they have a guilty secret. Typical activities, such as having friends visit their home, may be impossible due to the chaotic atmosphere. Some young people worry that they will grow up to be violent.

Children exposed to family violence are more likely to develop emotional or behavioral problems than those who are not. Some children and teens skip school, behave badly, or take risks to get attention. Children sometimes abuse drugs or alcohol or run away to escape the violence they experience or witness at home.

It's a fact: domestic violence

- One in every four women will experience domestic violence in her lifetime.
- About 85 percent of victims of domestic violence are women, according to the U.S. Bureau of Justice Statistics.
- Every day in the United States, more than three women are murdered by their husbands or boyfriends.
- Domestic violence is most common among women ages 16 to 24.
- According to the Department of Justice, more than half of domestic violence offenders abuse drugs or alcohol.

Some children who experience domestic violence try to cope alone. They may skip school rather than face their teachers and classmates.

Some victims of domestic violence are too scared to report the abuse or to leave a violent partner. They may be afraid for their own safety or that of their children. They may worry that they cannot afford to live on their own. Some victims of domestic violence hope that the abuse will end and that their relationship will improve. When domestic violence becomes a family secret, however, children get the message that violence is acceptable. As a result, they may never learn to form trusting relationships, or they may end up in violent relationships themselves.

Seeking help

Domestic violence should always be reported. Young people can get help and advice by contacting a helpline or by talking to an adult whom they trust—a relative, a teacher, a doctor, or a school counselor. Children should not try to stop the violence themselves. They could be hurt.

Family shelters

Many shelters offer temporary housing. Women and their

Women who experience domestic violence need to find a safe place for themselves and their children to stay.

children may live in a shelter or in an agency-owned apartment while they receive assistance and counseling. Some services are free. When there is a charge, the cost is usually dependent on a family's ability to pay.

Agencies and shelters usually offer support groups, job training, legal help, medical care, and mental health services or referrals for women who are victims of domestic violence. Children can usually receive group and individual counseling and education services. About half of residents in domestic violence shelters are children.

CASE STUDY

Jamie often heard his dad shouting at his mother. Sometimes the teenager heard dishes being thrown or smashed in the kitchen. Jamie didn't know what to do to help his mom. When he tried to stop the fighting, she shouted at him to get out of the room. Afterward he often saw that she was bruised or bleeding.

His mom never talked about the violent situation in their home. Jamie was worried that he would make even more trouble by telling someone. Every day, though, he was terrified that his mother was going to be killed.

Finally, Jamie spoke to a counselor at his school. She told him he didn't have to go through this experience alone. The counselor explained how Jamie could get help for his mom and himself.

At many domestic violence shelters, victims can get legal advice free of charge. Most shelters also offer counseling and other services to women and their children.

33

Bullying is a form of abuse that sometimes happens within families.

Child abuse

According to the World Health Organization, millions of children around the world experience abuse at home. Abusers can be parents, stepparents, brothers, sisters, other relatives, or caregivers.

The most common form of abuse is **neglect**. Neglect occurs when a child's basic needs for food, clothing, shelter, education, medical care, protection, and emotional care are not met. Neglect is usually observed by people who have close contact with children. Doctors, nurses, day care workers, relatives, and neighbors may see signs of neglect in very young children. Once children are in school, teachers often notice indicators of child neglect, such as poor **hygiene** or frequent absences.

Other forms of child abuse are physical abuse, sexual abuse, and emotional abuse. Physical abuse includes hitting, slapping, punching, biting, or burning a child. Sometimes physical abuse results from

In focus: bullying in families

Bullying is abusive behavior that can happen within families and at schools. Children can be bullied by parents, caregivers, brothers, sisters, other relatives, or peers.

Bullying can involve both physical and emotional abuse. Bullies sometimes hit or push their victims, call them names, tease them, or force them to do things they don't want to do. Young people who are bullied at home sometimes express their anger and hurt by bullying other students at school. Because they feel helpless at home, they try to control others in whatever way they can.

inappropriate or excessive physical discipline. An angry parent or caretaker may spank a child with enough force to cause injury.

Emotional abuse occurs when children and teens are not given needed love and approval. They may be constantly criticized, blamed, ridiculed, or threatened. They may be ignored, rejected, or isolated from friends and family members.

Sexual abuse occurs when someone is forced by another person into sexual acts or situations. Sexual abuse can happen to children or adults. In the United States, sexual activity of

Abusers may try to protect themselves by threatening their victims.

any kind between an adult and a person under a specific minimum age (which varies according to state law) is illegal.

In non-touching sexual abuse, a person may force a victim to look at sexual parts of the abuser's body or to watch sexual acts. Some sexual abusers force their victims to look at sexual images or videos. They may talk to their victims about sexual things in a way that is frightening or embarrassing.

Sexual abuse also includes forcing victims to touch others or to be touched in a way that makes them feel uncomfortable. **Rape** occurs when sexual intercourse is forced.

Sexual exploitation happens when abusers forcibly take sexually **explicit** photographs or videos of children. Children may also be forced to have sexual contact with people in exchange for money.

Emotional and physical harm

Abuse causes emotional harm as well as physical injuries. Children and teenagers who are constantly ignored, shamed, terrorized, or humiliated suffer as much as those who are physically abused. People who are bullied or abused can feel worthless, powerless, insecure, and alone. Sexual abuse can make victims feel guilty and ashamed, even though the abuse is never their fault.

Some young people who are abused engage in destructive acts, such as setting fires. They may abuse alcohol or drugs, have difficulty forming relationships, and withdraw from social activities. Some children start self-harming because abuse has made them feel ashamed or disgusted by their bodies. Others run away from home or even attempt suicide.

Taking action

Many abused children are reluctant to talk about the situation. They may worry about getting a parent or caregiver into trouble. Some abuse victims fear that they will be removed from their families and put into foster care. They may be afraid that others will not believe them.

Children who are experiencing any form of abuse should report it to someone they trust. This can be a relative, a teacher, a school counselor, a doctor, a coach, or a neighbor. Child care professionals, such as teachers and youth workers, must report the abuse so that the child gets appropriate help.

Children who feel afraid to approach someone in person can call a helpline and talk to a counselor in confidence.

Talking about abuse can be painful, but it is important that victims confide in others. Keeping a record of abusive incidents can help abused children recall them.

They will get information, advice, and support in reporting the abuse to authorities.

Children and teens may wish to keep a diary, noting every instance of bullying or abuse. By writing about the abuse, victims can gain some control over what is happening and how they feel about it. Written records can also help young people recall the abuse when they make a report.

Children who have experienced abuse may live with a foster family that can offer support while they recover.

It's a fact:
child abuse and neglect

- Approximately 40 million children younger than 15 suffer child abuse each year, according to the World Health Organization. Abusers are most often the child's parents.

- According to the U.S. Department of Health and Human Services, fewer than one-third of child abuse cases are reported.

- In 2005, at least 899,000 children in the United States were victims of abuse or neglect. Almost 17 percent of them said they had experienced physical abuse.

- More than half of the victims were seven years old or younger.

- In 2005, more than 40 percent of child abuse deaths in the United States were caused by neglect.

- Risk for neglect is highest among children younger than five years old.

- Each day, about four U.S. children die from abuse or neglect.

- More girls than boys are the victims of sexual abuse.

Chapter 6: *Child runaways*

Every year, millions of young people run away. Some run away from their families or stepfamilies; others flee foster homes or facilities where they have been placed because of family problems. One in seven kids between the ages of 10 and 18 will run away from home at least once. Most runaways are in their midteens, but some are younger. Children who run away when they are very young may do so repeatedly as they get older.

Family problems

Most children run away because of serious problems at home. Family conflict is the reason most frequently identified by callers to the National Runaway Switchboard crisis hotline.

Young people with problems at home may be vulnerable to online predators who pose as friends. Some teens have run away to be with strangers whom they met in a chat room or on a social networking site.

Family relationships are often strained at a time of crisis—for example, during a family breakup, after the death of a relative, or in the midst of serious financial problems.

About one in four children living in stepfamilies runs away by the age of 16. Competing for attention in a new family arrangement can leave children feeling neglected and vulnerable. They may also have problems getting along with a stepparent or stepsiblings.

Trauma and abuse

Approximately half of young runaways say they left home because of physical, emotional, or sexual abuse by a family member. Some children and teens run away because of drug or alcohol addiction problems in the family. Children may have witnessed domestic violence and want to escape the constant conflict at home.

Personal problems

Some runaways are trying to escape problems at school or with the police. They may have dropped out of school. Girls may run away because they are pregnant. Other teens run away to be with a girlfriend or a boyfriend, believing they can have a new life with that person. Some children leave home to meet up with a stranger they met online.

Big problems, bad choices

Many children and teens face tough problems—and there are ways to deal with all of these problems besides running away. Young people who think about running away may not know how to solve their problems. They may be frightened and desperate. Many of them do not have adults to turn to for help. They may think running away is their only choice. Unfortunately, the problems kids hope to escape by running away are replaced by other, even bigger problems of life on the street.

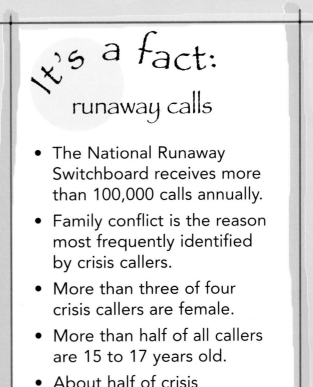

It's a fact:

runaway calls

- The National Runaway Switchboard receives more than 100,000 calls annually.
- Family conflict is the reason most frequently identified by crisis callers.
- More than three of four crisis callers are female.
- More than half of all callers are 15 to 17 years old.
- About half of crisis callers have been on the street for one week or less.

Some young people run away to escape their problems at home. Many of them face new problems, however, when they lack money, food, and a safe place to sleep.

Dangers and risks

Some young people run away for just a night and stay at a friend's house. They may want their parents to worry about them and to realize that they are unhappy. Other children and teens, however, run away with the intention of starting a new life for themselves. Many runaways end up homeless, living on the streets.

Crime and drug abuse

Child runaways face many dangers on the streets. They become tired, dirty, cold, hungry, and emotionally drained. Their health may suffer. Many runaways beg or steal so that they can get food to eat. Some of them suffer from **malnutrition**.

It's a fact:
living on the street

- From 1 million to 3 million young people are living on the streets in the United States.

- Girls are more likely than boys to seek help at shelters or to call hotlines.

- Nearly one-third of homeless children and teens have sold drugs to survive on the street.

- About one in five young people in homeless shelters has a drug or alcohol abuse problem. About 12 percent have thought about or attempted suicide.

Children who are living on the streets can be targeted by drug dealers. Some young people turn to drug dealing to earn money. Teenage runaways are five times as likely as their peers to abuse drugs and three times as likely to be in trouble with the police.

Many runaways are physically or sexually abused on the streets. One of every three teen runaways is lured into **prostitution** within two days of leaving home. About 300,000 young people are involved in prostitution in the United States. They are at risk for **sexually transmitted diseases**, unwanted pregnancies, and mental health problems.

Young people who run away from home may turn to shoplifting, selling drugs, or prostitution in exchange for money, food, and shelter.

CASE STUDY

Ronnie was 11 when he first ran away from home. He wanted to escape the constant fighting and violence between his mother and stepfather. Ronnie thought running away was his only hope of making his own life. He caught a bus to the city and tried to find a room in a cheap hotel, but he didn't have enough money. He spent the night under a bridge. The next day he wandered around a shopping mall and hung out in a video arcade.

The days stretched into weeks. When Ronnie was hungry, he begged for money. Eventually he turned to shoplifting. He was caught stealing, and the police contacted his mother. Ronnie went home, but the problems with his stepfather only became worse. Ronnie ran away again when he was 14. This time he met a drug dealer and began selling cocaine as a way of earning money to live.

Emergency shelters

There are more than 600 runaway shelters or housing facilities throughout the United States. They typically offer young people a bed, blankets, a shower, clothing, and food. Some shelters have family support workers and offer services such as counseling, substance abuse assistance, and health care for young people.

Runaway helplines

In the United States, a number of emergency hotlines can offer child and teen runaways immediate assistance, advice, and information. At the National Runaway Switchboard, for example, trained workers provide crisis intervention, referrals to local resources, and education and prevention services to young people and their families. The runaway hotline receives, on average, 100,000 calls a

In focus: help in an emergency

Some organizations offer emergency help for young runaways. Safe Place displays signs in libraries, fast-food restaurants, stores, and other businesses. A child or teenager can ask an employee to call Safe Place. A program volunteer will help the young person by providing shelter and counseling services.

year. The hotline operates 24 hours a day, 365 days a year. The National Runaway Switchboard also operates message relay and conference call programs to help young runaways who want to contact their parents.

The Boys Town National Hotline is a 24-hour crisis, resource, and referral line. In 2006, about 450,000 children and families were helped through the hotline. Trained counselors assist callers 24 hours a day, seven days a week.

The Covenant House NINELINE (800-999-9999) provides telephone crisis intervention to runaways and homeless children and their families.

Outreach workers seek out young people who are in danger on the streets and offer them information and assistance.

Callers have immediate access to crisis and counseling services.

Care and support

Some children and teens who have run away are unable to return home. They may have been forced to leave by a parent, or they may be afraid of returning to a home where they experienced domestic violence or abuse. These young people often need help from social workers to find foster care. Some organizations offer long-term programs that help 16- to 21-year-olds get education or job training, learn independent living skills, and find permanent housing. Some charities run **mentoring** programs to support child runaways.

Addressing problems

Some runaways want to return home but need practical help and support. With the assistance of the National Runaway Switchboard, the Greyhound bus line operates the Home Free program, which provides a free ride home for runaway children ages 12 to 18. Since the program began in 1984, it has helped about 30,000 runaways reunite with their families.

When young people return home, families need to address the problems that caused the children to run away. If family problems persist, family counseling or **mediation** can help resolve issues and prevent children and teens from leaving home again.

Counseling can help young people and their families deal with the problems that may have caused teens or children to run away.

Chapter 7: *Taking control*

When young people are having problems at home, they may not know where to turn for help. In some cases, they feel let down or betrayed by their parents or caregivers, and they no longer trust the adults in their lives. They may be embarrassed or ashamed to tell others about family problems. Some children are afraid of getting their parents into trouble if they seek help. However, young people should not have to cope alone with serious problems. There are people and organizations that can offer help and advice.

Talking it over

Talking to a trusted adult can help troubled young people feel better, think through their choices, and find solutions to the problems they are facing. Children and teenagers may choose to confide in a relative, a friend, or a neighbor.

Some schools provide counselors or peer support programs. Young people can also reach out to teachers, doctors, youth or social workers, and religious leaders. Youth crisis organizations can provide online, e-mail, or telephone support and advice.

Young people can seek and receive support through text messages and e-mail.

Personal space

Young people sometimes face problems that are beyond their control. As a result, they may feel powerless and lack self-esteem. Having time for themselves is important so that they don't feel overwhelmed by the situation and events around them.

Some children and teens keep a diary or a journal to express their feelings and understand the causes for their stress or depression. They may be helped by exercising or taking up a sport or a hobby on their own or with friends. Even spending time in places such as parks or libraries can provide a valuable outlet.

Most problems will not go away on their own. Young people need to know that other children experience

In focus: taking action!

If you know someone who is having a problem at home, you can offer support in many ways.

- Be a good listener. Let your friend talk to you in confidence, and don't judge. Be accepting and compassionate to help your friend feel safe.

- Involve the person in a new activity, such as a sport or a hobby.

- Offer to help your friend find people or organizations that can provide the help he or she needs.

- If you think someone is in danger or is being abused, tell an adult whom you trust.

similar problems and that people and organizations are available to help them. Even families that have gone through the most painful crises can heal, recover, and move forward by working together, accepting help, and supporting one another.

Being active is good for physical and mental well-being. Sports can help relieve stress and tension and boost mood.

Glossary

addiction: a compulsive need for and use of a habit-forming substance

Alzheimer's disease: a progressive disease of the brain that leads to impairment in memory, judgment, decision making, and language

antisocial behavior: actions that differ from socially accepted behavior. Antisocial behavior typically includes fighting, running away from home, abusing drugs or alcohol, and stealing.

anxiety: an extreme feeling of worry or fear

bereavement: the loss of a loved one by death

binge drink: consume several alcoholic drinks within a short time

blended families: families that include children of a previous marriage of one spouse or both

bullies: acts in an abusive, aggressive, and threatening way

counselors: people who are trained to provide support and advice

custody: legal responsibility for a child

depression: a mood disorder marked by sadness, inactivity, a significant increase or decrease in appetite and sleep, and feelings of hopelessness

domestic violence: physical or emotional injury by one family or household member of another

drug overdose: consumption of more than the recommended amount of a drug

endorphins: chemicals in the brain that produce a sense of well-being

eviction: removal of tenants from a property by legal action

explicit: very clear, obvious, or detailed

extended families: family units including uncles, aunts, grandparents, and other relatives

flashbacks: sudden, vivid recollection of a past incident

foster families: families that care for children born to other parents. A child may be placed in a foster family as the result of problems or challenges that are taking place within the birth family.

hospices: facilities that provide for the physical and emotional needs of people who are terminally ill

hygiene: practices to promote cleanliness and health

isolated: cut off from others

malnutrition: inadequate intake of nutrients

mediation: counseling designed to help ease conflict within a group

mentoring: the process by which an experienced person provides advice, support, and guidance to a less experienced person

neglect: failure to provide basic necessities such as food, shelter, and clothing

paramedics: specially trained medical technicians who provide a wide range of emergency services

parole: a conditional release of a prisoner

peers: people of the same age-group

probation: the act of giving a convicted offender freedom under the rules and supervision of a law enforcement officer

prostitution: engaging in sexual activity in exchange for money

rape: forced sexual intercourse

self-esteem: positive feelings about oneself

self-harm: actions, such as cutting or burning, by which people deliberately hurt themselves

sexual exploitation: victimizing or taking advantage of someone in a sexual way, usually for personal gain

sexually transmitted diseases: diseases, such as herpes, that are passed on through sexual contact

social workers: people who are professionally trained to help others with family, home, or social problems

stalking: harassment by repeated pursuit of or contact with a person

terminal illness: an illness that will cause death

therapeutic: providing or assisting in a cure

therapists: professionals trained to treat physical or mental problems

Further information

Books to read

Bishop, Keeley, and Penny Tripp. *Family Break-up* (Need to Know). Chicago: Heinemann Library, 2003.

Goodman, Marilyn E. *When a Friend Dies: A Book for Teens About Grieving and Healing*, rev. ed. Minneapolis, Minn.: Free Spirit Publishing, 2005.

Horsley, Heidi. *Teen Grief Relief*. Highland City, Fla.: Rainbow Books, 2007.

Veladota, Christina. *Teen Runaways* (Teen Issues). Farmington Hills, Mich.: Lucent Books, 2003.

Organizations to contact

National Domestic Violence Hotline
Web site: **www.ndvh.org**
Toll-free hotline: 800-799-SAFE (7233)
Hotline advocates are available 24 hours a day to provide crisis intervention, information, and referrals.

National Teen Dating Abuse Helpline
Web site: **www.loveisrespect.org**
Toll-free hotline: 866-331-9474
Teens can talk with a trained peer advocate 24 hours a day, seven days a week.

Childhelp USA
Web site: **www.childhelp.org**
Toll-free helpline: 1-800-4-A-CHILD (1-800-422-4453)
The child abuse hotline operates 24 hours a day, 365 days a year. All calls are anonymous.

National Runaway Switchboard
Web site: **www.1800runaway.org**
Toll-free crisis line: 800-621-4000

Helpful web sites

Teen Action Campaign/Family Violence Prevention Fund
www.seeitandstopit.org
"See It and Stop It!" is designed to educate young people about abusive relationships and to encourage them to take action.

TeensHealth
www.kidshealth.org
TeensHealth (part of the KidsHealth web site) provides teenagers and families with accurate, up-to-date information on running away and dealing with grief, divorce, stepfamilies, and abuse.

The Center for Grieving Children, Teens and Families.org
www.grievingchildren.org
Young people who are grieving a death can find help and information at this site.

Safe Place
nationalsafeplace.org
Safe Place provides access to immediate help and supportive resources for all young people in crisis. The Teen Topics section contains links, resources, statistics, and other information for runaways.

National Youth Violence Prevention Resource Center
www.safeyouth.org
This site provides information and resources on abuse, domestic violence, runaways, and teen dating violence.

Publisher's note to educators and parents: Our editors have carefully reviewed these web sites to ensure that they are suitable for children. Many web sites change frequently, however, and we cannot guarantee that a site's future contents will continue to meet our high standards of quality and educational value. Be advised that children should be closely supervised whenever they access the Internet.

Index